Flower Inspirations

By: P.C. Allaby

Be Still. Only in stillness will your questions be answered and your problems solved.

4

Feel the warmth of the sun on your face. That glorious feeling of aliveness is God within.

*When you feel bliss,
you are in
alignment with
the Universal Plan.*

Know that you are
never alone. God
is within you and
you are within
God's embrace.

Every human being, flower, tree and all matter in the entire universe is energy from the same source.

*Be compassionate.
What you do to
others, you do to
yourself.*

Look closely at a
flower. Instead of
with eyes, see it
with your heart.

True compassion heals. Only with light, does a shadow disappear.

On an exhalation
release all
negativity. Repress
all retorts and
negative thoughts
and breathe in the
joy of being alive.

*It is not necessary
to always be right.
Instead, be silent
and know truth.*

Be. You do not need to do anything more. You are already enough.

You are a being of
God; perfection
without having to
be perfect.

26

Each of us is like a square on a patchwork quilt. One missing patch and the quilt cannot be complete. We are all necessary.

Be careful with words you think or speak. They create.

There is no need to strive or struggle. When you are doing what the Universe planned, life is filled with joy.

*Do not fear death.
It is leaving this
form to know your
eternal being.*

The Universe knocks. It is up to us to open the door.

Tending a garden with loving hands does more to bring harmony to our world than rallying against injustice.

Riling or
protesting against
something will
only cause it to
expand. Instead,
pray for
compassion and
light.

A good friend is
like a prayer being
answered.

Love is the most precious gift of the Universe.

Give gratitude and receive joy.

Made in the USA
Charleston, SC
15 September 2015